# INQUIRY ILPs
## Individualized Learning Plans
## for Life-Based Inquiry

The Instructional Design Library

*Volume 11*

# INQUIRY ILPs
# Individualized Learning Plans
# for Life-Based Inquiry

Philip G. Kapfer
*University of Utah*
*Salt Lake City*

and

Miriam Bierbaum Kapfer
*University of Utah*
*Salt Lake City*

Danny G. Langdon
*Series Editor*

**Educational Technology Publications**
**Englewood Cliffs, New Jersey 07632**

**Library of Congress Cataloging in Publication Data**

Kapfer, Philip G
    Inquiry ILPs.

    (The Instructional design library; v. no. 11)
    Bibliography: p.
    1. Individualized instruction. 2. Study, Method
of. I. Kapfer, Miriam B., joint author. II. Title.
III. Series.
LB1031.K347    371.39'4    77-25438
ISBN 0-87778-115-X

Printed in the United States of America.

Library of Congress Catalog Card Number: 77-25438.

International Standard Book Number: 0-87778-115-X.

First Printing: February, 1978.

To
Asahel D. Woodruff,
colleague and friend

# FOREWORD

The ILP is a clear example of the fact that an individualized instructional design need not have rigidly fixed content that must be prepared in advance and then "prescribed" for a student by the teacher. Instructional designs *do* include those learning strategies that unfold as students and teachers use them. Such designs unfold, however, through careful direction and planning.

The most impressive characteristic of the ILP approach is that it involves learning processes that require the *student* to unfold them. Learning episodes are not simply given to the student; he or she must "make it happen" by participating in the structuring of learning. This is not to suggest that the student is left to wander by himself. As the authors clearly state, "The processes of learning need to be 'taught' as surely and as thoroughly as the subject matter content that those processes are designed to expose." I am particularly delighted to note that the authors of the ILP approach suggest how this can be done in a straightforward, "no nonsense" manner.

You will notice, as I did, in the Operational Description section of this book, that the authors deal in some detail with their view of "how people learn," that is, with concept formation. I found that this amount of background or "theory" was essential in order to later understand how Inquiry ILPs match the requirements of concept formation. Therefore, take the time to read every word and to carefully examine the illustrations. If you want students to learn more than "knowledge" or "content," the ILP instructional designs described here have much to offer you.

Danny G. Langdon
Series Editor

# PREFACE

This book on inquiry-type learning presents two "Individualized Learning Plans" (ILPs) that have resulted from a decade of work on life-based education in the Life-Involvement Model (LIM) Project, initiated by Asahel D. Woodruff and currently co-directed by the authors. Two other ILP instructional designs, for project-type learning, are published as a separate volume in this series.

In most conventional instructional designs, the student has two sources for learning about any given subject matter, namely a textbook and a teacher. The school-wise student studies both of these. The textbook is studied for the author's mainly verbalized concepts about the objects and events that comprise the subject matter. The teacher is studied primarily for the purpose of determining which of these verbalized concepts should be memorized because of the likelihood of their turning up on a test.

This learning game is called "school." When played under conventional rules, it is a dependency-developing game in which the student depends on the teacher to decide what is important to learn. Given the fact that most individuals are conditioned by 12 to 20 years of experience at playing this basically debilitating game, it is little wonder that virtually every occupation or profession has problems with the continuing education of its members.

Two learning games normally played *outside* of school are (1) open-ended inquiry, and (2) inquiry that is focused by the demands of in-life goals. These latter two learning games might just as well be played *inside* school, and in this book we are suggesting exactly that. If this were done, the development in schools of efficient and self-reliant life-long learners could become the rule rather than the exception.

The two instructional designs presented in this book—the Exploration ILP and the Competence ILP—"carry" the two life-based inquiry processes just mentioned. The ILP designs tie together subject matter content, learning resources, and productive ways for the learner to "find out and know," both now and in the future.

P.G.K.
M.B.K.

# CONTENTS

# ABSTRACT

### INQUIRY ILPs
### Individualized Learning Plans
### for Life-Based Inquiry

Two Individualized Learning Plan (ILP) designs for life-based inquiry are presented. The first was developed to promote *open-ended inquiry* and, therefore, is descriptively titled an "Exploration ILP." The second design—the "Competence ILP"—also was descriptively titled based on its emphasis on *focused inquiry* aimed at the development of specific mental and performance competencies (such as the competencies needed for rationally choosing goals and for achieving them effectively).

ILPs are not learning resources in themselves. Rather, ILPs "carry" the *life-based inquiry processes* that bring together for the student the subject matter content and learning resources. ILPs may be teacher-constructed or student-constructed, although the latter is described by the authors as having the greater potential for meeting individual differences.

Individualizing instruction with ILPs means giving the learner the *freedom*, the *structure*, and the *responsibility* for selecting subject matter content according to learner wants and needs. ILPs may include the use of realia and any kind of print or non-print media. The learning activities that may be used with ILPs include large-group and small-group instruction, laboratory exercises and experiments, tutoring and coaching on a one-to-one basis, student learning teams, independent study, or any combination of these and other instructional arrangements.

Finally, ILPs may be used with all levels of students, from primary age children who are able to use reading as a learning tool, all the way to students enrolled in advanced technical, professional, and scholarly programs of study. That is, Exploration ILPs may be used whenever students have a "want-to-know," and Competence ILPs may be used whenever students have a "need-to-know."

# INQUIRY ILPs
## Individualized Learning Plans
## for Life-Based Inquiry

# I.

# USE

The central idea that is basic to the use of Individualized Learning Plans (ILPs) is straightforward. For effective and efficient individualization of instruction to take place on an ongoing, self-sustaining, and systematic basis, some sort of ILP is needed. The ILP simply *carries the inquiry processes* that bring subject matter content and learning resources* together for the learner. Thus, an ILP is *not* a learning resource in itself; it is an organizer.

ILPs obviously may be either teacher-constructed or student-constructed. *Teacher-constructed ILPs* direct students to pre-determined learning resources that focus on pre-determined subject matter content. This is fine for certain purposes. However, the fullest potential of the ILP as a device for individualizing instruction is reached in the *student-constructed* form of the ILP. Achievement of that full potential depends, of course, on the extent to which the student has learned the processes of inquiry that underlie the ILP. Therefore, a critically important teacher responsibility is to help the student to increasingly understand and practice the processes of inquiry.

*Learning resources, in our view, include (1) human resources such as faculty, peers, students, clients, and patients; (2) realia such as artifacts, models, and natural phenomena; and (3) media including both print and non-print formats. These learning resources may be made available in school or community settings.

Because a central idea in this book is "individualization," we should clarify at the outset just what we do and do not mean by this term. Hitchens (1974) sought to explain this concept by itemizing a number of *common misconceptions* about individualization. In reading through the following paraphrased list, please remember that these are the commonly *mis*understood extremes to which a functional program for individualization does *not* usefully go:

(1)   Every student must work alone (e.g., independent study).

(2)   Carrels are necessary.

(3)   Audio-visual materials must be used.

(4)   Individualized instruction works only in (a) someone else's subject, (b) at some level other than the level at which I teach, (c) with smaller classes than mine, (d) etc.

(5)   Individualized instruction is inflexible.

(6)   Individualized instruction has to involve a massive system of shelved materials that form the basis for teacher-prescribed instruction.

(7)   Individualized instruction is complete freedom for the students to do as he or she chooses.

(8)   Students have no idea of what is "good" for them.

(9)   Students always know what is "good" for them.

Stated now in a *positive* way, individualized instruction *does* commonly include the following elements:

(1)   Provision for variability among students in the *rate* at which they are able to achieve a desired degree of mastery of a given behavior.

(2)   Provision for variability among students in the *"skills"* (e.g., reading, writing, using audio-visual equipment, etc.)

that they possess at a given point in time, and, therefore, their readiness for employing these skills as tools for using various learning materials and activities.

(3) Provision for variability among students in their knowledge, understanding, and attitude development along a continuum ranging from simple perception to the highest levels of understanding and value development (choice of action).

(4) Provision for variability among students in their *verbal development* (e.g., ranging from "show and tell" to understandably communicating complex ideas).

(5) Provision for variability among students in their *motor skill development* (e.g., ranging from random movement to using precision, control, grace, or speed of movement).

(6) Provision for variability among students in *responsibility development* (e.g., self-direction, self-initiative, self-discipline, willingness to put forth effort, or willingness to follow oral or written instructions and standard operating procedures) along a continuum from external (teacher) shaping of these behaviors to conscious (student) valuing and choosing of these behaviors.

(7) Provision for variability among students in readiness for *self-motivated learning* (e.g., based on immediate academic, in-life, or career goals that each student wants). (Kapfer and Kapfer, 1972.)

At the same time, in individualized instructional materials and activities, concern is commonly demonstrated for one or more of the following elements:

(1) Provision for variability in societal, parental, and student *expectations* concerning the subject matter and behaviors to be learned.

(2) Provision for variability in *interactions* among students, between students and teachers, and between students and materials.

(3) Provision for variability of *subject matter* in forms (from concrete to abstract) and in formats (books, films, objects, discussions, etc.) that most efficiently and effectively support the behaviors being sought.

(4) Provision for variability in *instructional settings* (whether for individual students or for groups of students) in which interactions can take place, subject matter can be learned, and behavior can be practiced.

(5) Provision for the *motivational appeal* of the interactions, materials, and settings (Kapfer and Kapfer, 1972).

To summarize, individualizing instruction means giving the learner options according to his or her needs.

The particular ILP instructional designs presented in this book were developed for use by teachers and students working together, as well as for independent use by students. In a teacher-and-student setting, nothing in the way of "tools of learning" except a functional reading ability is required in order to use the ILP designs effectively, because the designs are intended to represent how people *naturally* go about learning in different situations. If the ILP designs are used independently of a teacher, however, the student also should possess selected "independent study" abilities. The exact nature of these abilities would vary with the previous experiences of the student, with the subject matter being learned, and with the learning resources available and their location.

### Two Kinds of Inquiry ILPs

We have limited ourselves in this book to instructional designs for "inquiry" of two kinds. First, there is the kind of *open-ended inquiry* in which a topic—some object or event—has been identified and the student's purpose is to learn something about that topic.* Examples of open-ended inquiry topics might include the following: "exercise," "values," "empathy," "colloquialisms," "taxes," "birds," "proteins," "fabrics," "CB radios," "acrylics," "surrealism," "melody," "numerals," "sensory receptors," "texture," and the like. (Of course, these topics as just listed are actually *classes* of objects and events, and would be made concrete and specific at the start of or within an actual inquiry experience.) Open-ended inquiry of the type suggested here results from a *want* to know. The instructional design for open-ended inquiry is called an "Exploration ILP."

The second instructional design that is presented in this book involves the kind of *focused inquiry* that results from a *need* to know. The instructional design for focused inquiry is called a "Competence ILP." The same topics as those listed in the last paragraph may be involved, but this time with a different orientation. A "competence" is now involved in which such objects must be *used* competently (or such events *carried out* competently) because they now are means for achieving some end. Examples of competencies include (1) carrying out an *exercise* program in order to strengthen a weak back; (2) determining whether or not *proteins* are being excreted by the body in order to identify a patient's physical problem; or (3) mixing *acrylics* in order to achieve just the right hue for a painting. Thus, this second kind of inquiry or instructional design gets at functional learning in which the payoff is some desired product for which the new competence is needed.

---

*By "learn something," we mean to gain knowledge and understanding about the subject's *properties of structure* (i.e., size, shape, composition, steps to follow), *properties of function* (i.e., what the object and its parts do or what outcomes are anticipated from an event), and/or *properties of quality* (i.e., color, texture, and other structural-type properties that do not contribute to function).

The two instructional designs presented in this book will work effectively in many types of teaching-learning situations. For example, inquiry ILPs have been used successfully at the primary level in elementary schools, at the advanced levels of medical school, and at most levels in between. They can be adapted easily to fit unique ways of expressing the critical steps involved in particular learning processes, and to match the specific behaviors and subject matter content being taught. Some teachers have used inquiry ILPs for group-paced instruction by using a generous diversity of learning resources to meet individual needs. Others have used the designs to facilitate totally student-planned inquiry. An expanded list of situations in which inquiry ILPs can be used includes the following:

(1) teacher-initiated or student-initiated content;

(2) teacher-planned or student-planned learning experiences;

(3) teacher-pacing or student-pacing;

(4) beginning or advanced levels of content;

(5) classroom and interaction-oriented learning activities, or library and community-based independent study;

(6) concrete or abstract subject matter content; and

(7) factual subject matter content or generalizations and principles.

In spite of all this flexibility, our very strong bias is that students should be given the freedom to engage in much of their own planning for learning. However, freedom must be tied to structure. In other words, freedom is meaningless unless the teacher provides the structures that expose alternatives (where alternatives exist) and that guide student action (where action is indicated). The two instructional designs presented here provide the structure that students need for guiding their learning actions—that is, for guiding the inquiry processes in which they engage. As a result, teachers may focus as much student attention as they wish on the *processes* of inquiry in their subject matter areas, as well as on the *content* that is being studied.

**Appropriate Content for Inquiry ILPs**

Now let us look at the kinds of content that may be used with inquiry ILPs. Three kinds of content organization will be illustrated. The first of these is the most familiar kind because it is found frequently in textbooks in the form of indexes and tables of contents. Gross categories, objects, events, and sub-divisions are listed. Careful *analysis* is the major technique used in organizing content in this way. In the examples given below, the teacher or author begins with a class of objects or events (or a specific object or event) and analyzes it into its component parts, as follows:

*Language Arts*
I. The Formal Letter
  A. Heading
    1. Street address
      a. Building number
      b. Street name
    2. Name of city or town
    3. Name of state and zip code
    4. Date
      a. Day
      b. Month
      c. Year
  B. Inside address
    1. Etc.

*Science/Auto Mechanics*
I. Automobile
  A. Engine
    1. Ignition system

     a. Distributor
      (1) Points
        (a) Etc.

*Chemistry*
I. Titration Equipment
  A. Burette
    1. Stopcock
      a. Stopcock grease
        (1) Etc.

*Medicine*
I. Digestive Tract
  A. Gastric secretion
    1. Enzymes
      a. Pepsin
        (1) Pepsinogen
          (a) Etc.

In contrast with the above examples, in which analysis was used to "take apart" an object or event, a related technique for developing content outlines is that of *generation*. In this case, increasingly specific categories are generated from a single large category, as follows:

*Psychology of Learning*
I. Motivation: Action Starters
  A. Starters *within* tasks themselves
    1. Provocative issues
    2. Attractive goals
  B. Sense-perceivable things
    1. Physical
    2. Aesthetic
    3. Etc.
  C. Reminders of and clues to previous experience
    1. Concepts
    2. Feelings
  D. Formal controls
    1. Rules
    2. Prescriptions
    3. Assignments
    4. Directions

      5. Physical manipulations
      6. Commands
      7. Physical force
   E. Informal expectations
      1. Customs
      2. Mores
      3. Opinions
      4. Suggestions
      5. Respectable ideas
   F. Conditioning influences
      1. Positive reinforcers
         a. Approval
         b. Pay
         c. Intrinsically satisfying results
      2. Negative reinforcers
         a. Social
         b. Tangible
         c. Intrinsic
      3. Nonreinforcement (Woodruff and Kapfer, 1973)

A third kind of content organization reflects a concern for the steps in *problem-solving*. Content organized in this way contains the actions that must be taken and the subject matter that must be understood in order to solve problems. This kind of content organization is found often in professional fields such as law and medicine. The content outline may be in the form of a problem-solving flow chart or algorithm, as in the example from medical education (Tolman and Kapfer, 1976) shown in Figure 1.* The obvious intent is for the student to learn the designated medical content within the context of diagnosing the cause of a patient's problem.

The chances are very good that the teacher reading this book already has an outline in mind for what he or she wants

*From a psychological point of view, such algorithms are "mental constructs" formed on the basis of repeated diagnoses of the same problem. For this reason, such algorithms may differ from one physician to another.

*Figure 1*

*Dysphagia Curriculum Content*

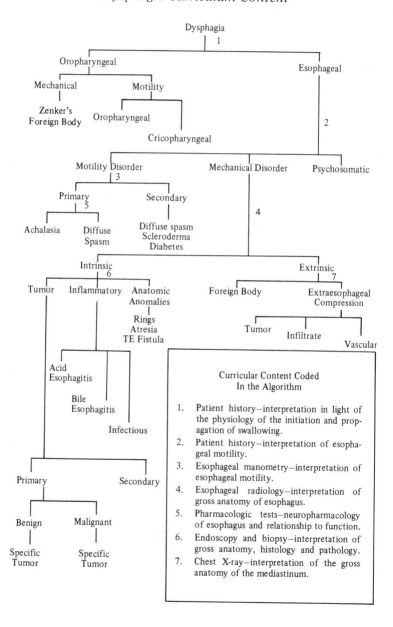

to teach. The nature of that outline will depend on any number of factors ranging from what the teacher expects the student to do with the content to the manner in which the content is handled in the teacher's favorite textbook on the subject. In any case, the three techniques for organizing course content just presented are adequate for demonstrating the kinds of content that may be used with the two inquiry ILP designs presented here.

## References
### *(USE section)*

Hitchens, H. Individualizing Instruction: Introduction to the Theme of the Month. *Audiovisual Instruction*, May 1974, *19* (5), 6.

Kapfer, P. G. and M. B. Kapfer. Introduction to Learning Packages. In *Learning Packages in American Education*, pp. 3-10. Edited by P. G. Kapfer and M. B. Kapfer. Englewood Cliffs, New Jersey: Educational Technology Publications, 1972.

Tolman, K. G. and P. G. Kapfer. Dysphagia Curriculum Content. Unpublished algorithm, 1976.

Woodruff, A. D. and P. G. Kapfer. A Life-Involvement Teacher Education Curriculum: The Scope Pattern. Unpublished paper, 1973, pp. 20-24.

# II.

# OPERATIONAL DESCRIPTION

The operational description of any instructional design is dependent upon the instructional designer's unique view of how people learn. In the case of the Inquiry ILPs being presented here, the learning approach is called "concept formation." *That is, we are concerned with how the teacher, through ILPs and supporting teaching strategies, can arrange the student's environment for the most efficient and useful learning of new concepts.* In order to deal with concept formation within the ILP teaching-learning design, we will discuss very briefly in the next several paragraphs (1) the different levels of concepts that are encompassed by this word, and (2) the ways in which these different kinds of concepts are formed.

### Concept Formation in Inquiry ILPs

*Mental imagery.* The concept-forming process involves *sensory intake* (experiential learning) that results in the formation of "mental imagery." Concepts can change, and usually do with added experience. The more experience we have with a given object or event, the more we will recognize and understand about it, and the clearer our "mental imagery" will become. Verbal labels may be assigned, of course, to the objects and events upon which such non-verbal concepts are based. Simply stated, "Words are the names we give our experiences" (Dale, 1976). Obviously, such verbal labels often are memorized (e.g., "tonic chord," "dominant 7th chord," "subdominant chord," etc.).

*Generalized concepts.* The sensory intake process is followed by an automatic mental process that results, over time, in the *association* of various specific mental images, thereby forming "generalized concepts." The teacher may promote this process of generalization and make it more efficient by causing the student to recall his or her related mental images, to identify common properties of structure, function, and/or quality,* and to associate these mental images in the form of generalizations. Generalizations also may be given verbal labels to be memorized. (For example, "music," "weather," "trees," "chemicals," "nations," "grammar," "watercolors," and so forth are all verbal labels for more or less inclusive generalizations.)

*Principles and "laws."* When *events* instead of objects are generalized, we call them *processes*. For example, "campaigning for elective office" is a phrase that describes a "process," rather than a specific campaign "event." Another example is "mixing acids and bases" (the process) and "mixing a given amount of HCl and NaOH" (one specific event). When generalized process concepts attain sufficient reliability, we further elevate them to the level of a *principle* (an "If ..., then ..." concept), the most stable of which we call *laws*. For example, "If the demand for a given item exceeds the supply, then its value (e.g., price) will increase."

*Mental constructs.* The generalizations and principles that we construct through our thinking processes also end up, for all practical purposes, as specific mental pictures. We call these thought-constructed pictures "mental constructs."

*Phenomena appear to have only three types of "characteristics" that we have called properties of *structure, function*, and *quality*. Please see the footnote on p. 7 for a fuller definition of these properties.

For example, mathematical models that describe the probability of finding an electron at a given point in space around the nucleus of an atom are highly abstracted from reality. However, the chemistry teacher knows that s, p, d, f, g orbital theory, which is based on these abstract mathematical probabilities, can be taught in concrete, sense-perceivable form by using drawings and models. The resulting mental imagery allows chemistry students to predict certain chemical and physical events, and thus provides a functional level of conceptualization. The abstract symbolic information about orbital theory that is the basis for such models may be memorized, if necessary, even down to algorithms for the probability calculations. However, such memorization is usually most effective if the abstractions are memorized in direct association with their representations.

*Symbols (language).* The symbolic components of concepts, such as verbal labels, have already been mentioned. However, the frequent use of written materials in the place of perceptual media is a continuing problem in schools. Therefore, to re-emphasize what has been said already, *the concept formation approach to learning depends upon extensive exposure of the student to a wide variety of natural and man-made phenomena (objects and events).* Predominantly symbolic (e.g., verbal) media and human interactions are used for the tasks of (1) associating symbols with already formed concepts, and (2) comparing concepts in teacher-learner groups.*

*Feelings.* Feelings, together with the values and preferences those feelings produce, are associated inescapably with every concept. Obviously, this "affective" component of learning cannot be separated from the "cognitive" components of

---

*This is in contrast to "information processing" approaches, in which verbal propositions rather than perceptual experiences are the primary tools for concept learning.

*meaning* (understanding) and *symbols* (language). Therefore, it is very important that the student's encounters with a given phenomenon be associated with positive feelings that will increase the chances of the student valuing that particular object or event. For example, the career-oriented student is more likely to have positive feelings (or at least neutral ones) if a given subject matter is learned in very close association with the manner in which it is to be used on the job—that is, if it is learned in a "relevant" manner. Other factors that affect the "feelings" component of concept learning include (1) the degree to which the learner has a choice of subject matter; (2) the use of an evaluation plan that is consistent with objectives; (3) the extent to which learning resources are convenient and useful; and (4) the efficiency of the learner's personal inquiry approaches.

This, in highly abbreviated form, is the way in which concept formation operates. This view of the place of concept formation in learning has a *direct relationship* to the content and shape of the two Inquiry ILP designs presented in this book. In the following sections, an overview is given of how the ILP designs, operating in school settings, are used to promote concept formation.

**The Exploration ILP**

The Exploration ILP, as the name implies, is designed to remind students of the steps they may take when exploring in an open-ended way the properties or characteristics of a phenomenon (an object or event). The "behavioral objective" for such inquiry could be written as follows: "You (the student) will be able to demonstrate in whatever manner you choose what you have learned." This objective puts the student on notice that he or she is in school to *learn*. At the same time, the objective indicates a recognition of the psychological fact that perceptions will differ among students even when examining the same properties of a given phenomenon. This is true because the learner always combines newly acquired perceptions of a given phenomenon with his or her own unique *prior* perceptions of the same and other phenomena, and, therefore, forms a new concept that is probably somewhat different from anyone else's.

The Exploration ILP has a little of the "Everest complex" in it—the wish to study something "because it is there." And this is acceptable to most teachers, at least for general education purposes. The difficult part for many teachers in using Exploration ILPs is to learn to step aside long enough *to let the student engage in personal inquiry to the point of curiosity satisfaction.* Curiosity satisfaction is a powerful reinforcer and is the natural consequence of successful inquiry. This is *not* to say that the teacher has a hands-off role, especially if the student is having difficulty that becomes counter-productive to continued learning. The point is that while the student is studying some object or event, his or her attention *should be on the properties of that object or event and not on the teacher.* The teacher's primary role in the early stages of inquiry, therefore, is to help the student focus his or her attention on *a given phenomenon* as such, on as many *examples* as possible of the phenomenon, and on the basic *properties* of the phenomenon.

Verbal interaction about the phenomenon being studied may occur after the student has had enough perceptual experience with the phenomenon to make "concept checking" meaningful and useful. Such interaction should occur at this stage (and probably not sooner) in order to reduce the danger of teacher-student interaction becoming a "school game" in which the student is trying to figure out "what the teacher wants to hear." If interaction is forced when students have not really had sufficient inquiry time to learn anything, they will have nothing about which to "concept check."

*Open-ended inquiry processes.* What did we mean when we said earlier that the Exploration ILP format is designed to remind students of the steps they may take during the open exploration of an object or event? First, we do *not* mean that there is a prescribed series of steps that always must be taken for concept formation (learning) to occur. On the other hand, it is obvious that any given inquiry experience will indeed involve a series of steps, and that, although these steps may differ considerably from one inquiry episode to another, we can generalize many such inquiry episodes in order to identify the common processes that are often involved. The Exploration ILP, therefore, is a *guide* for the student's inquiry, not a recipe for thoughtless step-following.

The student may begin an inquiry experience by formulating questions. The questions may be simple or complex. Knowing how to ask questions at several levels (such as "remembering," "understanding," and "thinking") is a useful inquiry tool. More sophisticated students might learn to apply Bloom's (1956) six taxonomy levels to their inquiry questions.

Another useful inquiry tool for students is an understanding of the three "properties" of phenomena that were mentioned earlier—structure, function, and quality. If the student understands the nature of these three kinds of properties, he or she will have an exceedingly valuable tool for the open exploration of his or her environment. Objects that are static, such as a house, are most likely to be examined by the immature inquirer for *structural* properties. The more sophisticated learner, however, quickly starts thinking about the *functional* properties of even static objects. He or she also examines more closely certain structural and functional properties that do not have independent existence, such as "color," "squareness," "coziness," "ranch style," etc., and identifies these as properties of *quality*. In such activity, the student is using a basic mental process in concept formation—the process of *differentiating among the things observed*.

A third inquiry tool for students is the ability to pair the "property" being studied with the appropriate sensory channel (e.g., eyes, ears, etc.) so that a match is achieved between the "messages" that the property sends and the sensory "receiver." To use a well-worn example, perfume requires *smelling*, and all the *looking* in the world will not reveal its aromatic properties. Furthermore, the student should realize that the type of sensual media that is most effective in transmitting information is dependent upon the type of information to be transmitted.

The properties of certain phenomena can be experienced only vicariously. For example, few of us have personally experienced the ground and air vibration of a Saturn V rocket taking off from Kennedy Space Center. But certainly we can get a "feel" for the experience from the visual coverage on television, from the associated audio coverage, and from the verbal descriptions of news personnel that remind us of our own past experiences. Thus, the ideal of an exact match between "message" and sense channel "receiver" may be compromised by the realization that partial experience is better than no experience at all.

The final inquiry tool to be mentioned here is "retention theory"—how to memorize and remember information most efficiently (at the point in the ILP at which verbal labels must be applied to newly acquired concepts, generalizations, and principles). For example, "massed practice" at remembering symbols or words followed by intermittent practice periods would usually result in better retention than would a single practice session containing the same total amount of practice time.

### The Competence ILP

A number of the characteristics of Exploration and Competence ILPs are the same. Both involve concept formation. Both are inquiry-based learning episodes. Both result in mental as well as overt performance competencies. There are, however, two primary factors that distinguish the Exploration ILP from the Competence ILP. First, the motivational basis for learning differs; in the case of the Exploration ILP, motivation is based on curiosity, while in the Competence ILP it is based on a need to know. Second, in the Exploration ILP the inquiry may lead in any direction, while the inquiry in the Competence ILP is sharply focused by the anticipated use of the newly acquired competence.

*Competence.* By "competence," we mean what the student is able to *do* with the phenomena that are involved in choosing and achieving his or her goals. The *doing* may be covert (mental or cognitive effort) or overt (verbal or nonverbal performance), as required. The statement of the competence on the ILP format generally will reveal what kind of competence is involved (covert, overt, or both) and what may be required for its achievement. It is of greater importance, however, that the student views the competence *within the context of its use* and wishes to be able to apply the competence in that context. In other words, the designated competence must be at a level of inclusiveness that is *motivationally sound.* For example, "Reading poetry aloud" is a competence goal written at a sound motivational level for many people. Conversely, the competence of "Identifying, in examples of poetry, specific instances of trimeter, tetrameter, and pentameter" probably is not of burning interest to many of us. Learning the meaning of such technical terms in poetry may indeed result from one's study while learning to read poems, and this is fine, but such terms are generally too atomistic to be "relevant" *as competence goals* in our instructional design.

*Focused inquiry.* The student's understanding of the nature of the competence will increase as he or she begins to expose and study the phenomena that are involved in the competence. To continue with the poetry example, a beginning poetry reader might plan and carry out the following focused inquiry steps for identifying phenomena for study:

(1) listen to a poem recorded by a competent poem reader;

(2) record the same poem;

(3) compare the two recordings for the purpose of diagnosing the differences;

(4) scan a book on "the art of poem reading" to identify the phenomena involved (e.g., subject, theme, and meaning; rhythm, meter, and sound; speaker, speaker's situation, audience, and tone; etc.);

(5) study in detail one or more of these phenomena;

(6) practice reading the same poem using the newly acquired knowledge; and

(7) solicit feedback or coaching from a teacher or peers.

This same series of steps, or some other series, may be repeated any number of times until the student achieves an acceptable level of competence in poetry reading.

*Evaluation.* Evaluation of student learning in Competence ILPs should center on three kinds of outcomes:

(1) Can the student identify and describe the essential phenomena that are involved in performing the competence?

(2) Does the student have a functional grasp of the properties that are critical for using each phenomenon in performing the competence?

(3) Can the student "get it all together" and actually perform the competence within the context of its legitimate use?

The teacher is responsible for making sure that the student knows what phenomena, if any, are "minimum requirements" for performing the competence. This may be accomplished through any one of the following means:

(1)   use of completely teacher-constructed Competence ILPs;

(2)   use of effective one-to-one or small-group counseling with students who are engaged in self-constructed Competence ILPs;

(3)   use of some type of "content index" provided to students who self-construct Competence ILPs; or

(4)   use of an actual self-evaluation system provided to students as they both initiate and complete self-constructed Competence ILPs.

By these means, the competencies that students gain may be specified as loosely or as stringently as the teacher may wish. The teacher should be clearly in charge, of course, to insure that appropriate mastery standards are defined and met.

## References
*(OPERATIONAL DESCRIPTION section)*

Bloom, B. S. (Ed.). *Taxonomy of Educational Objectives, Handbook I: Cognitive Domain.* New York: David McKay Company, Inc., 1956.

Dale, E. Message from Edgar Dale. *EducatioNews,* July 1976, *1*(1), 2.

# III.

# DESIGN FORMAT

Formats for the two Inquiry ILP designs presented in this book are described and illustrated in this section. The first of these was developed for *open-ended* inquiry and, therefore, was descriptively titled, "Exploration ILP." In this design, the idea of curiosity satisfaction is paramount. The second ILP design was developed for *focused* inquiry and also was descriptively titled, "Competence ILP." The latter design emphasizes the development of the particular mental and performance competencies that are needed for choosing and achieving one's goals. The basic components of these two kinds of Inquiry ILPs are shown in outline form in Figure 2.

### Exploration ILP

As indicated in Figure 2, Exploration ILPs contain the following four basic parts: (1) the name of the object or event being studied; (2) a list of open inquiry questions concerning the study topic; (3) a list of anticipated learning activities and resources; and (4) a student summary of the content that was learned. These four parts may be arranged sequentially as headings on a single sheet of paper, with appropriate space between headings to accommodate teacher or student responses, while planning or carrying out an open-ended inquiry episode. Each of the four parts of the Exploration ILP format will be discussed and illustrated in the

*Figure 2*

*Inquiry ILP Format Outlines*

| **Exploration ILP: Format Outline** |
|---|
| 1. *Object or Event*<br>    (i.e., phenomenon, thing,<br>    subject, topic)<br><br>2. *Inquiry Questions*<br><br>3. *Learning Activities and*<br>    *Resources*<br><br>4. *Student Summary of What*<br>    *was Learned* |

| **Competence ILP: Format Outline** |
|---|
| 1. *Competence*<br><br>2. *Description or Outline*<br>    (of the subject matter<br>    involved in performing<br>    the competence)<br><br>3. *Learning Activities and*<br>    *Resources*<br><br>4. *Test* |

following four sub-sections. A complete example of this instructional design is provided in a final sub-section.

*Object or event.* The first section of the Exploration ILP is headed simply by "Object or Event." Other relatively synonymous headings could be used, such as "phenomenon," "thing," or "topic." The name of the phenomenon that is chosen for study is recorded in this section of the format.

If students are permitted to select for themselves the phenomena for their study, then obviously the potential curricular content from which to choose must be revealed to students in some appropriate form. Means for effectively exposing potential subject matter content to students are of several types. One possible approach, assuming that the phenomena in a given area can be represented visually, is a *pictorial index.* Another possible approach is to allow *natural and man-made objects* to serve as direct sources of interest stimulation (such as would result from frequent and regular visits to a natural history museum or an art gallery). For more experienced students, *written indexes* such as the ones included in the "USE" section of this book may be useful. Such written indexes would cause recall of past experiences with the listed phenomena and thus would perhaps result in the selection for study of specific phenomena from the list.

Teachers at the elementary school level frequently reveal alternatives to children by introducing a broad topic and then helping the children select for individualized study one or more of the specific phenomena within that broad category. In fact, this approach to revealing potential content for study is useful at almost any educational level, as can be seen in the following example. Using the broad curricular topic "food" as an introduction at the elementary level, individual children might select for exploration one or more of the following: "meats," "vegetables," "cereals," "milk products," "fruits and berries," "eggs," etc. More advanced students could inquire at increasingly atomistic levels by exploring "proteins," "fats," "carbohydrates," "minerals," "vitamins," etc. Further analysis of this subject would yield a virtual abundance of smaller topics for increasingly advanced levels of study, even through the level of graduate research in nutrition.

The commitments of teachers and students when using Exploration ILPs go well beyond the simple actions of teachers *providing* some kind of content index and students *selecting* from it. The teacher also is responsible for creating the entire set of conditions (i.e., the environment) in which student motivational states are changed so that "want-to-know" and "need-to-know" learning take place on an ongoing basis. The students, on the other hand, are responsible for experiencing (i.e., opening up to) the environment provided by the teacher. Anything short of these two parallel commitments will adversely affect both teaching and learning. Teachers and students will have to be willing to "work at it" if they want the kind of freedom of choice that is the obvious consequence of the ILP approach suggested here.

*Inquiry questions.* A nine-year-old boy was asked to sort through a group of fifty photographs and select the one that most interested him. He selected a picture of a person water-skiing with a hang-kite. Although the set of photos was developed for different purposes (Educational Insights, Inc., 1975), each one did include questions on the reverse side that are somewhat similar to the inquiry questions in an Exploration ILP. The questions related to the hang-kite water-skiing photo were as follows:

(1)   How do you think this sport started?

(2)   Do you think it will be very popular in the future? Why?

(3)   How do you think this person became interested in hang-kite water-skiing?

(4) What do you think goes through his mind just before he lands?

(5) If you were steering the boat, what things would you have to be careful of?

(6) Have you ever been in a power boat? Would you like to?

Having read the above questions and having looked at the photo again, the nine-year-old wrote the following three additional questions:

(1) How high in the air do you go when hang-kite water-skiing?

(2) How fast does the boat have to go to lift you off the water?

(3) About what weight do you have to be to get off the water?

Some of the questions in these two sets are better inquiry questions than others, of course. At least two of the questions may be answered with a simple yes-or-no, and as a result these items may have limited value for generating thoughtful inquiry. The last item in the second set of questions may deserve a high rating to the extent that it indicates a healthy level of *personal* motivation for inquiring into the properties of the phenomenon called "hang-kite water-skiing." Other tools for examining and improving upon inquiry questions include a number of classification schemes, such as (1) the type of "property" being exposed by the questions, (2) the level of cognition required by the questions, and (3) the subject matter "scope" coverage that would result from inquiry based on all of the questions. These three tools will be discussed briefly in the next paragraphs.

In an earlier section of this book, we mentioned the three kinds of "properties" exhibited by phenomena—those of structure, function, and quality. Students at practically any level can learn to ask questions that get at these three types of properties. Using these categories, how would one classify the two sets of questions about hang-kite water-skiing? Or would such classification depend on a fuller discussion of the personal meaning to the student of each of the questions? For example, the question "How do you think this sport started?" could refer to the *structure* of the event (the steps that were taken) that caused the introduction of hang-kite water-skiing as a sport. Or, the question could reveal the *function* of the news media, sports enthusiasts, athletic clubs, sporting goods stores, and the like in promoting hang-kite water-skiing. Or, the question could refer to the *quality* of life when "fully lived" because of the closeness of physical danger, thus providing the essential motivation for the sport to take hold and stay.

Using the same two sets of questions as examples, a second way to classify them is to ask whether all of the questions are simple fact-type questions or whether some of them require more thoughtful responses. In our view, most of the hang-kite questions are at the lower levels of Bloom's (1956) taxonomy (i.e., knowledge and comprehension), and probably should be supplemented by additional questions that get at all six levels of the taxonomy. The contents of Figure 3 are designed to assist in analyzing the inquiry questions in an Exploration ILP to determine their verbal-cognitive levels. Even elementary school children can learn to classify questions using this table.

A third way of looking at inquiry questions in Exploration ILPs is from the perspective of different classifications of subject matter. Using a mixture of conventional and non-traditional subjects, and "the moon" as a topic, the following questions demonstrate a wide range of types of content:

## *Figure 3*

### *Improving Inquiry Questions in Exploration ILPs*
### *Using Taxonomic Schemes*

| Bloom's Taxonomy Classifications | Taxonomy of Related *Overt* Behaviors | | Taxonomy of Related *Covert* Behaviors |
|---|---|---|---|
| Knowledge | Acquire<br>Define<br>Distinguish | Identify<br>Recall<br>Recognize | Remembering |
| Comprehension | Demonstrate<br>Differentiate<br>Illustrate<br>Interpret<br>Make | Rearrange<br>Represent<br>Rephrase<br>Translate<br>Transform | Understanding |
| Application | Apply<br>Choose<br>Classify<br>Develop<br>Employ | Generalize<br>Organize<br>Relate<br>Restructure<br>Transfer | |
| Analysis | Analyze<br>Categorize<br>Classify<br>Compare<br>Deduce | Detect<br>Discriminate<br>Distinguish<br>Identify<br>Recognize | Thinking |
| Synthesis | Combine<br>Design<br>Develop<br>Formulate<br>Modify | Originate<br>Plan<br>Specify<br>Synthesize<br>Tell | |
| Evaluation | Appraise<br>Argue<br>Assess<br>Compare<br>Consider | Contrast<br>Decide<br>Judge<br>Standardize<br>Validate | |

(1)  From the perspective of *oneself*: "How does a full moon make me feel?"

(2)  From the perspective of *interpersonal relationships*: "What is the effect of the moon on the courting behavior of Homo sapiens?"

(3)  From the perspective of *physics*: "What happens to light coming from a distant star that passes near the moon?"

(4)  From the perspective of *literature*: "What are some of the great stories that include the moon as a central component?"

(5)  From the perspective of *biophysics*: "How does the light from the moon stimulate one's sensory perception systems?"

(6)  From the perspective of *mathematics*: "How does one calculate the mass of the moon?"

(7)  From the perspective of the *fine arts*: "What are some of the possible ways that dancers in a modern dance company could represent the phases of the moon?"

Using whatever subject matter classification scheme that may appeal, the teacher should examine the student's inquiry questions for a specific Exploration ILP (such as the two sets of "hang-kite water-skiing" questions just provided) for their "fit" within the chosen classification scheme, being sure that no gaps in subject matter coverage occur over a given period of time.

To summarize, one of the most important responsibilities of the teacher in using Exploration ILPs is to help the student develop his or her questioning abilities. The student's initial inquiry questions may be answered, refined, or replaced by different questions as he or she progresses in an inquiry experience. (This would be the case whether the questions came from a published source, from the teacher, or solely from the student.) The teacher should help each student learn to ask inquiry questions that are *meaningful* (to the student) and that serve to *expose the properties* of the phenomenon being studied. The student, on the other hand, is responsible for *identifying* what he or she wants to learn about the phenomenon through the questions that are asked.

*Learning activities and resources.* Exposing the properties of a phenomenon, such as happens in an Exploration ILP, involves the process of analysis. This is done in two ways—by means of open inquiry questions (discussed in the previous section) and by developing appropriate learning activities and resources. In other words, through the inquiry questions that are asked and the learning activities and resources that are used, an object or event is taken apart piece by piece (actually or mentally) so that the individual parts that make up the object or the steps that comprise an event can be perceived. The inquiry process of exposing the properties of a phenomenon is not, of course, restricted to natural and man-made physical objects. "Music," "poetry," "drama," "football," "fly fishing," and the like all have properties of structure, function, and quality, and many of these properties must be exposed if the student is to gain some degree of understanding of events involving these phenomena.

Because some things cannot be seen directly or taken apart physically (at least with the expectation of putting them back together again), media must be found that perform this service. Thus, teachers and students must learn to search out media in the form of schematics, diagrams, cutaway pictures, etc., that expose the properties of the phenomenon being studied.

For example, a "four cycle gasoline engine" in an automobile is at least superficially familiar to most of us. The properties of such an engine and of all of its individual parts, however, probably would require some new learning for most people. Many teachers assume that an ideal learning situation in this or similar cases is to provide the student with direct hands-on experience with the real thing. It is often further assumed that the learning situation could be made even more ideal by providing an expert automobile mechanic-educator to work with students on a one-to-one or small-group basis. Research indicates, however, that *initial* direct hands-on experience with the real thing is not always the best way to learn. On many occasions, it is better to encounter a phenomenon for the first time, particularly a complicated one, in a well-designed mediated form that simplifies the student's encounter by removing extraneous distractors. Direct hands-on experience and tutoring *subsequent* to such mediated experience may then be very appropriate and profitable for the student.

Another example of learning activities and resources for a possible inquiry topic may be useful. "Flower" is the name we use for a generalized concept that includes all of the varieties of blossoms produced by plants, shrubs, trees, and so forth. If a student is studying "flowers," then he or she may interact with that phenomenon by using print and non-print media of various kinds, as well as by direct perceptual experiences with specific flowers. Diagrams of flowers in books will be helpful as will time-lapse films in which the opening and closing of flowers, methods of pollination, the functions of flower parts, etc., can be viewed. The teacher can facilitate all of these learning activities by being concerned with questions such as the following:

(1) Has the student interacted with specific examples of the phenomenon ("flowers" in this case), using appropriate media to facilitate his perception?

(2) Has the student perceived the sensuous properties of the phenomenon?

(3) Has the student stored some conceptual memory of those properties?

(4) Can the student talk about what he learned by calling upon his memory of the phenomenon and by associating the correct vocabulary with the phenomenon?

To conclude, the purpose of the learning activities and resources in an Exploration ILP is to assist the student in gaining an increased understanding of the things that make up the environment. The most important responsibility of both the teacher and the student is to make sure that *conceptualization* actually takes place, rather than rote memorization of data or of someone else's verbalizations of concepts.

*Student summary of what was learned.* Students should have opportunities throughout the learning activities in their Exploration ILPs to summarize what they have learned and to communicate their perceptions to each other and to the teacher. It is quite possible, of course, for a student to completely miss certain properties of a phenomenon and to perceive other properties inaccurately. In order to avoid such "mis-learning," continuous checking of concepts should occur. Such on-going evaluation both re-directs the student's learning efforts and leaves him well-prepared for the final evaluation session.

An example of the importance of "concept checking" and verbalizing what has been learned is shown by the following event. A group of giraffe pictures were drawn by very young children who had been taken on a field trip to the zoo to see various animals. In a sense, the pictures represented a "summary" of "what was learned" at the zoo's giraffe house. In producing the pictures, the children were asked to draw the giraffes that they had just seen, but they were not given an opportunity to discuss their zoo experiences prior to the drawing task. The children exhibited considerable discomfort with this task and produced highly variable and inaccurate pictures. Subsequently, the children were asked to draw pictures of zebras, but only after having had an opportunity to freely discuss the group of zebras also housed at the zoo. The discussion session gave the children a chance to check and communicate their perceptions with each other and with the teacher before beginning the second drawing task. The resulting zebra pictures were far more accurate representations than were the giraffe drawings and, more importantly, they were drawn with enthusiasm and delight. Thus, although communicating one's perceptions may not contribute to an entirely quiet classroom or library, the psychological facts about learning tell us that communicating one's perceptions is absolutely essential both to the concept formation process and to its affective components.

To conclude, if all of the feedback and interaction opportunities inherent in Exploration ILPs were actually capitalized upon during the planning and doing of an Exploration ILP, there would be less need for a final student summation of what was learned. However, given customarily large classes at most educational levels, many teachers cannot expect to provide all of the one-to-one and small-group consultations with each student that would be desirable. Thus, in addition to periodic teacher-student discussions, the student needs to pull together his or her learning into a well-coordinated whole for final presentation to the teacher and/or peers. This summation of work provides the student with valuable practice at organizing and presenting material that is meaningful to him, and it doubles as an end-of-ILP evaluation session.

*An example of an Exploration ILP.* In the preceding discussion of each of the four basic parts of the Exploration ILP format, a variety of topics was used for illustrative purposes (including "food," "hang-kite water-skiing," "the moon," "four cycle gasoline engine," "flower," "giraffe," etc.). These several topics were useful for showing the *flexibility* in content and instructional levels that can be accommodated within the Exploration ILP format. One additional example, employing a single topic throughout, will serve to further clarify the use of the format. Figure 4 consists of a "teacher-constructed" Exploration ILP on "Nonverbal Communication," a topic of wide interest and appeal. The sample ILP in Figure 4 is not tied to a particular age or grade level because the actual content involved would be determined by (1) each student's "want-to-know" level, and (2) each student's experience at interacting directly with this content, his skills at perceiving and exposing the critical properties of the content, and his ability to associate appropriate vocabulary with those properties and remember them.

## Competence ILP

As was indicated earlier, in Figure 2, Competence ILPs contain the following four parts: (1) a statement of the competence that the student wishes to develop; (2) a description or outline of the subject matter involved in performing the desired competence; (3) a list of anticipated learning activities and resources; and (4) some type of "test" of the student's ability to demonstrate the desired competence. As with the Exploration ILP, these four parts may be arranged sequentially as headings on a single sheet of paper, with appropriate spacing between them for teacher or student responses. Such "format sheets" then may be used by the teacher for designing Competence ILPs for students, or by students themselves for planning and guidance in carrying out their own focused inquiry experiences.

Each of the four parts of the Competence ILP will be discussed in the following four sub-sections. Rather than using a number of different curricular topics for illustrative purposes, we will focus on a single topic throughout our

*Figure 4*

*Exploration ILP on "Nonverbal Communication"*

**Exploration ILP**

*Object or Event*: Nonverbal Communication
(Nonverbal communication refers here to any message sent by a person that is *not* written or spoken.)

*Inquiry Questions*: (What do you want to learn about the phenomenon?)

(1)    You are accustomed to "reading" the nonverbal communication of others. But how *accurate* are you at "people reading"? In other words, do you usually see consistency among the various verbal and nonverbal cue patterns exhibited by others? If not, why not?

(2)    How do you think you come across nonverbally to people who are older than you are? To your age peers? To people who are younger than you are? In a retail sales situation? In a classroom situation when you are the student? When you are the teacher?

(3)    What techniques can you acquire that promote a "match" between your intent and your nonverbal messages?

(4)    How can the physical environment (of an office, for example) be arranged to transmit messages of trust, openness, concern, happiness, calm, etc.?

(5)    In a political campaign, what is the significance or value in terms of potential votes of presenting positive "body language" (subtle nonverbal cues that reflect honesty, intelligence, industriousness, and other desirable qualities)?

(6)    Etc.

*Learning Activities and Resources*:

(1)    *View*: 35 mm. slides on the topic "Nonverbal Communication and Facial Expression." This series of slides shows examples of the nonverbal communication of teachers, with an emphasis on the use of facial expressions and head gestures.

*(Continued on next page)*

*Figure 4 (Continued)*

(2) *Read*: Use at least four articles and/or one book published during the past five years on the topic of nonverbal communication. (These materials may be pre-identified by the teacher, or they may be totally student researched and selected.) Discuss with other students your understanding of the ideas you gained through reading, and the meaning of these ideas in terms of the slides you viewed in the first learning activity.

(3) *Do*: Visit five classrooms, offices, stores, waiting rooms, hotel lobbies, etc. (if possible, when the users of such places are not present). What does the use of space in these places communicate to you? Look for such things as arrangement of furniture and appointments, placement of lighting, use of color and texture, and use of directional aids.

(4) *View*: Videotape on "Nonverbal Communication in an Office Setting." This is a videotape of credit officers at a finance company interviewing potential borrowers. First view the tape with the sound turned off. Try to determine the messages being communicated nonverbally by both categories of people. Check for agreement with a fellow student. Does your interpretation of the nonverbal communication agree with that of your partner? If there are areas of considerable disagreement, replay the tape, stopping at those points where you do not agree. Examine the specific behavior about which you disagree.

(5) *Do*: Examine your own nonverbal behavior by making a five to eight minute videotape of yourself working with a small group of people in a discussion setting. The objective of your activity is to get the group to talk about something of interest to them. After the discussion, play the videotape without sound, and observe your own nonverbal communication. Analyze the types of nonverbal cues that you seem to use most frequently. Play the tape a second time. Now observe and categorize the nonverbal reactions of

*(Continued on next page)*

*Figure 4 (Continued)*

members of the group to each other and to you. Play the
tape a third time for one or more of your fellow students,
and concept-check with them concerning the nonverbal
messages being sent and received.

(6)   Etc.

*Student Summary of What was Learned*: Depending on your previous
experience and professional focus (e.g., elementary or high school
student, undergraduate teacher education student, in-service
teacher, college professor, political campaigner, physician in practice, shopkeeper, etc.), you might prepare a report or do a project
that illustrates the impact of the content of this ILP on your immediate day-to-day life. Other options would be equally valid, as
long as they relate to your individual "want-to-know" situation in
life.

discussion of the Competence ILP format—the competence of "collecting information." This topic is useful because it has applications at almost all levels and kinds of schooling. It can be used for learning to collect information for a primary-level classroom newspaper, for interviewing a customer regarding repair of the customer's automobile, for eliciting information from a patient regarding a physical complaint, and for a host of other types and levels of information gathering needs. A complete "teacher-constructed" high school level Competence ILP on the skills involved in "interviewing" will conclude this section.

*Competence.* Competence is the ability of a person to perform an act that is involved in achieving some goal. The act may be a mental one, a motor skill, an operant response, or a verbal act. Each of the task steps (means) for achieving a goal (end) qualifies as such an ability (competence).

The most critical aspect of stating a competence, whether this is done by the teacher or by the student, is to determine the level of inclusiveness that the student can handle. For example, one of the competencies required for producing a classroom newspaper is to "collect information for news articles." This ability may be usefully defined to include the following sub-set of student competencies:

The student will be able to ...

(1) Interview school people in one-to-one situations.

(2) Take notes at school meetings.

(3) Describe school incidents in narrative form.

(4) Verbalize impressionistic school data.

(5) Collect demographic school data.

(6) Etc.

The level of inclusiveness employed in competence statements should not be higher than the student's current potential for achievement. That is, it should identify for the student any act that he or she can realistically be expected to learn to perform.

*Description or outline of the subject matter involved.* This section of the Competence ILP includes two related activities. First, an *analysis* of the *competence* must be carried out so that the phenomena are identified upon which the student must "act" competently. If the Competence ILP is not teacher-constructed, the student may need to engage in learning activities in order to perform this analysis. In such cases, the teacher should be concerned with how completely and accurately the student has analyzed the competence. For example, when collecting information for news articles, the following minimal number of phenomena probably will be involved: (1) news, (2) the news collecting process, and (3) accuracy. Other phenomena, such as "the research process," may be added later in order to further mature the basic competence for more experienced learners.

Second, the *properties* of the phenomena that are critical for mastering the competence *must be identified.* That is, each phenomenon identified above has critical properties with which the student must be, or become, familiar. The exposure of these critical properties is necessary in order for the student to learn about them. The teacher should determine how well (or completely) the critical properties were discovered and exposed in a student-constructed Competence ILP. For example, the phenomenon, "the interview process," may be dealt with as though it has only functional (or process) properties, such as (1) preparation for the interview, (2) beginning the interview (establishing rapport), (3) conducting the interview, and (4) recording the interview. For a beginner's purposes, Items 2, 3, and 4 may be the *critical* properties. Other properties, such as (1) the number and length of interviews, (2) the interviewer's sensitivity to the needs of the interviewee, (3) the physical setting for the interview, (4) the interviewer's reputation, and (5) the interviewer's knowledge of the interview topic, may be ignored under certain circumstances until the interviewer is motivated to mature his interviewing behavior by adding these and other properties.

To summarize these two activities related to describing the subject matter in a Competence ILP: first, the desired *competence* is *analyzed* for the *phenomena* that are involved; and, second, the *phenomena* are *analyzed* for their *critical properties*. The critical properties, then, are the level at which the student begins his study.

*Learning activities and resources.* As just indicated, the critical properties (of the phenomena involved in the desired competence) now become the subject matter for focused inquiry. The result of this learning should be a functional understanding of how the phenomena behave so that the student can use the phenomena competently. For example, as listed above, one of the phenomena in the competence of collecting information for news articles is "the interview process." The *critical* properties of this phenomenon were identified as (1) beginning the interview, (2) conducting the interview, and (3) recording the interview. At this point in the student's progress through the Competence ILP, he or she must learn how these three critical properties of the interview process operate or behave. For example, information of a factual or objective nature usually can be secured by direct questions, but information of a purely personal or confidential nature may have to be obtained indirectly. The person being interviewed may recoil from the thought of revealing certain types of information too openly or directly. And the interviewer may not know the significance of certain details that may have been avoided or ignored. By attending to specific *critical properties* of the interview process, the interviewer can develop the skills for coping effectively in such interview situations.

While all of the learning processes or steps discussed thus far are being carried out by the student, he or she should be communicating with others (peers, teachers, parents, and/or resource persons) in order to (1) check perceptions and conceptual interpretations, (2) recall prior perceptions and concepts, (3) obtain feedback concerning operational decisions for engaging in inquiry and for carrying out that inquiry, and (4) obtain feedback to help insure full and accurate perceptions of the consequences of his or her inquiry decisions and activities. Obviously, effective communication of this sort also requires that the student engage in learning activities and resources that result in the student learning the *vocabulary* related to the phenomena that are involved in the desired competence. For example, possible interview-related terms such as "interview theme," "interviewer focus," "interviewee profile," "follow-up question," "off-the-record response," etc., are the type of vocabulary items for which student mastery at the appropriate level would be needed.

Finally, the learning activities and resources for any competence should include practice of that competence in realistic situations. Conceptual and verbal inquiry are essential, of course, but they cannot take the place of actual practice and guidance in acquiring the necessary ability to perform. The competence must be practiced until its performance is good enough to facilitate achievement of the goal for which the competence is being learned. For example, the student could practice gathering information for a newspaper article by interviewing fellow students. In order to achieve maximum student gains in interviewing effectiveness, the teacher or whatever media is used may point out that interviewing draws heavily on knowledge provided by the social sciences, particularly concepts dealing with the individual and his reaction to the environment. The interviewer must understand the respondent as a person. At the same time, the interviewer must understand himself as a person. The insightful teacher can help the student perceive such interrelationships, but must be very careful not to force the student into "wouldn't it be nice to know" learning that the student does not perceive as being functional for the desired interviewer competence at the student's current level of maturity.

*Test.* At the conclusion of the Competence ILP, the student should verbalize what he or she has learned, either orally or in writing, to the teacher or some equivalent person. Such communication improves the student's learning and, for many students, can be structured to demonstrate that learning has taken place at the appropriate cognitive levels of (1) knowledge, (2) comprehension, (3) application, (4) analysis, (5) synthesis, and (6) evaluation. In addition, such teacher-student discussion can also be planned to investigate whether or not the learning experience was satisfying (the affective component of the student's learning). One such "test" is described in the following paragraphs. It will be noted that this "test" is not at all like the traditional paper-and-pencil type of test for measuring learning.

For example, a student may view a filmed episode of someone conducting an interview, or the student may read a typescript of an interview. Subsequent student study of this material and discussion of it with the teacher may result in the student differentiating between interviewer questions that were prepared in advance and questions that resulted from on-the-spot follow-up of leads that were revealed during the interview. "Knowledge," "comprehension," and "application" of other subtle but discernible interviewer techniques also may be demonstrated at this point.

The discussion with the teacher, as described thus far, may have raised the student's understanding to the level of "analysis." Subsequent work could result in the student's (1) "synthesizing" the parts of the sample interview in such a way as to reveal a pattern or structure not evident before, and (2) "evaluating" the sample interview by developing or using criteria for judging its effectiveness. The teacher should remain aware of the fact that the student's feelings (the affective component) toward the content of his learning (the interview process, in this case) accompany each level of cognitive learning and become involved in how the student perceives each level.

The "test" is completed, of course, when the student is able to demonstrate satisfactorily his or her competence in either a simulated or a real-life situation. The demonstration may be an audiotape or videotape of the student interviewing someone. It may come directly from work done during the learning activities and resources part of the Competence ILP, or by re-creating such an interview for the "test" situation. Either method of student demonstration of the competence is acceptable because, in the Competence ILP, the desired *behavior* or competence must be congruent with both the *practice* of that behavior and its *evaluation*.

*An example of a Competence ILP.* In the preceding paragraphs, each of the four parts of the Competence ILP format was illustrated using various aspects of the competence of "collecting information." As indicated earlier, we will now "put it all together" in a single format. A "teacher-constructed" Competence ILP that focuses on interviewing skills for the high school journalism student is presented in Figure 5.

## Figure 5

*Competence ILP on "Collecting Information by Interviewing"*

**Competence ILP**

*Competence*: Collecting Information by Interviewing (for a high school journalism project)

*Outline*:
(1) Phenomenon: The interview process.
(2) Properties of the phenomenon:
  (a) Preparation for the interview.
  (b) Beginning the interview (establishing rapport).
  (c) Conducting the interview.
  (d) Recording the interview.
  (e) Closing the interview.

*Learning Activities and Resources*:
(1) View network and local news programs (especially in-depth news presentations) for interviews conducted by professional news reporters. Record the audio portion of several such interviews. Select the interview that you think is best and analyze it carefully for the parts of the interview process that it contains.

(2) Use the library to locate material dealing with the interview process. This phenomenon will be dealt with at varying levels of difficulty in subject matter areas as diverse as journalism, sociology, clinical psychology, personnel management, sales, and the like. Your task in this learning activity is to further expose the *breadth* and *depth* of properties of the interview process. For example, additional properties at the same level as those already listed in the above outline might provide greater *breadth* of content for study: (a) the number and length of interviews, (b) the interviewer's sensitivity to the needs of the interviewee, and (c) the interviewer's reputation.

Greater *depth* is illustrated by the following properties that could be listed on the outline as sub-parts of "Preparation for the interview": (a) the physical setting for the interview, and (b) the interviewer's knowledge of the interview topic.

*(Continued on next page)*

*Figure 5 (Continued)*

Sub-parts of "Conducting the inverview" might include the following: (a) direct questions for obtaining factual or objective information, and (b) indirect questions for securing information of a personal or confidential nature.

*What other properties could provide additional breadth or depth? Which of these are critical properties that you must be able to handle competently while "collecting information by interviewing"?*

(3)   Participate in discussions with fellow students and with your teacher as you develop and expand the content outline of properties of the interview process. Clarify and adjust your outline as necessary.

(4)   Study the properties that you have identified as *critical* for your understanding of the interview process. Use the media that you located during the second learning activity as resources for your intensive study.

(5)   With the help of fellow students, practice interviewing in a journalism setting. At some point, you may wish to produce audiotapes or videotapes of these practice sessions in order to analyze your performance and in order to seek informed feedback from peers and from your teacher.

(6)   Etc.

*Test:*

(1)   Bring two copies of your content outline to a scheduled "laboratory" session. Provide the teacher with one of the copies. The teacher will show a filmed episode of a well-known journalist conducting an interview with a world leader. Analyze the interview for the properties involved. Then participate in a class discussion based on a comparison of your analysis of the filmed interview with the properties you listed as you expanded your content outline for this ILP.

*(Continued on next page)*

*Figure 5 (Continued)*

(2)    Bring one of your own videotaped interviewing episodes to a "laboratory" session. It will be analyzed by at least two of your peers with participation by your teacher. An evaluation checklist will be provided for this activity. The checklist will be signed by you and the peer evaluators before being turned in to your teacher.

**Inquiry ILPs and Teacher Roles**

Both kinds of Inquiry ILPs presented in this book require of the student three essential steps as follows:

(1)   *Task Starting*: The student focuses his or her attention on a segment of the potential subject matter of the "course."

(2)   *Task Focus*: The student studies that subject matter using teaching-learning resources including other people, natural things, artifacts, and print and non-print media.

(3)   *Task Completion*: The student "wraps up" his or her work in some useful way and self-evaluates it.

This sequence of steps occurs whether the student is using ILPs or is involved in highly conventional lecture-recitation approaches to teaching and learning. These three steps may appear deceptively self-evident—and perhaps even superficial. Closer inspection of them, however, will reveal them to be at the heart of successful learning episodes. In this section, therefore, we will examine the teacher's role when using ILP designs as that role relates to task starting, task focus, and task completion.

*Task starting.* In the vernacular we say, "How can I motivate a student?" In actual fact, we are really asking how we can create conditions that cause the student to change his or her *own* motivational state. Teachers and students have differing responsibilities in the teaching-learning act, and it helps to know *who* is responsible for *what* in any joint venture.

The working climate and related teacher-student commitment to learning tasks that is established in a classroom is largely a function of the teacher's behavior. Student behavior is also an important factor in climate, of course. But it is the teacher and not the student who is responsible for climate-setting behaviors such as the following (Woodruff, 1969):

(1) providing clear and stimulating explanations of the significance of the tasks in which students are expected to engage;

(2) establishing warm teacher-student rapport through personal reactions to students that indicate appropriate approval, acceptance, affection, compassion, and interest;

(3) detecting and alleviating gaps in the student competencies needed for engaging in realistic and efficient learning;

(4) communicating to students the teacher's own commitment to learning about the subject matter;

(5) establishing a learning environment that recognizes individual differences among students; and

(6) reinforcing student behaviors that contribute positively to a serious-minded and enjoyable working climate.

Quite obviously, a classroom climate characterized by the behaviors just described is an action-starting kind of atmosphere in which to work.

With the climate factor as a "given," we will now look at other, more specific kinds of task-starting help for students. The most obvious and most important task starter in open-ended inquiry, such as occurs in Exploration ILPs, is *the thing itself that is to be studied*. In focused inquiry, such as in Competence ILPs, the *goal to be achieved* must be sufficiently satisfying to "carry" the competence that is to be gained. We call both of these "starters within tasks themselves." Another way of expressing this is with the overworked word, "relevance." An object or event can be "relevant" to a student if he or she is curious about that object or event. A competence, on the other hand, is *not* relevant in and of itself. Rather, a competence becomes relevant if it is perceived as a means for achieving a desired end. For example, competence in (1) editing written material, (2) shooting baskets, or (3) recognizing the eight danger signals of cancer may be "relevant" to given individuals as these three competencies ("means") relate to the "ends" of (1) producing a publishable book, (2) winning a basketball game, or (3) maintaining one's health. In other words, competencies should be taught in direct association with their use so that the natural motivation of that use can "carry" the focused inquiry necessary to acquire the competence.

Other sometimes necessary but less desirable task starters that the teacher may use include: (1) *formal controls*, such as entrance requirements, tests, grades, promotion requirements, certification and licensing requirements, etc.; and (2) *conditioning influences*, such as are found in behavior modification approaches to classroom control (see Smith and Kapfer, 1972, for a thorough discussion of conditioning influences and their relationship to the implementation of individualized instructional programs). Teachers should view these two types of action starters as supportive of rather than as central to their motivational task with students. Once an individualized program using ILPs has been operating reasonably well for a few months, most task starters should be *within* the learning tasks themselves.

*Task focus.* In most conventional instructional designs, the student learns about any given subject matter by focusing on a textbook and a teacher. The student's task focus in an ILP is very different from that just described. The student's attention is focused (1) on a *phenomenon* (an actual object or event) rather than primarily on information such as a textbook author's concepts about something, and (2) on the *processes* of exposing and learning about the properties of that phenomenon rather than on the teacher's ideas of what

should be learned. We will discuss these two focuses—
*phenomenon-focus* and *process-focus*—one at a time.

As discussed earlier, phenomena have properties of structure, function, and quality. In Exploration ILPs, any or all
of these properties are appropriate for student-task focus.
In Competence ILPs, the student attends *only* to those
properties that must be understood in order to perform
competently. (Of course, the student may *wish* to pay
attention to non-essential properties, but this would clearly
become exploration-type inquiry.) In both kinds of inquiry,
the teacher's principal role is to facilitate the learner-task
focus. This is accomplished (1) by orienting students to the
resources that are available to them and supervising their
use of that resource system, and (2) by teacher-student
interaction. The latter is for the purpose of comparing newly
formed concepts. Such "concept checking" is accomplished
by means of teacher behaviors, such as the following (expanded from Woodruff and Taylor, 1969):

(1)   Requiring student identification of a phenomenon that is
      present, and student differentiation between it and other
      similar and dissimilar phenomena.

(2)   Requiring student identification of the properties of a
      phenomenon that is present, and student differentiation
      among its properties of structure, function, and quality.

(3)   Requiring student description of a phenomenon that is
      present and its properties.

(4)   Requiring student recall of phenomena that are not present
      (but that have been perceived before) and their properties.

(5)   Requiring student organization or reorganization of phe-
      nomena and/or properties to form a new concept.

(6)   Requiring student prediction of the consequences of an
      event.

According to Woodruff and Taylor (1969), each of the above six "eliciting behaviors" of the teacher may result in one or more of the following student responses: (1) perceiving, (2) describing, (3) analyzing, (4) reviewing and organizing, (5) interpreting and explaining, (6) concluding, and (7) predicting consequences.*

In addition to promoting the *phenomenon-focus* just described, the teacher's role in an ILP system also includes helping students to focus their attention on the *processes* of learning. The basic inquiry processes in Exploration and Competence ILPs are indicated by the four headings on each of the two ILP formats (see Figure 2, p. 26). These headings can be greatly expanded in terms of meaning, of course, as was done in the preceding two major sections (pp. 25-49). It should be clear that students need to be "taught" these inquiry processes in reasonably sized increments, followed by practice of the processes with appropriate corrective feedback. Any teacher, regardless of level, who assumes at the outset that his students are already competent at performing open-ended or focused inquiry should carefully re-examine his assumptions. *The processes of learning need to be "taught" as surely and as thoroughly as the subject matter content that those processes are designed to expose.*

*Task completion.* The traditional role of the teacher as an evaluator is a familiar but not always comfortable one. In an ILP system, the evaluation role of the teacher is somewhat different. The primary question now becomes, "How can the teacher help students learn to *self*-evaluate their own learning

---

*By way of contrast, the conventional teacher spends considerable time and effort dispensing verbal information, e.g., describing, giving data, stating conclusions, stating predictions, and stating moral precepts (Woodruff and Taylor, 1969). The conventional teacher also spends considerable time seeking verbalistic responses that indicate that the information just dispensed is being memorized.

honestly, realistically, and usefully?" The first step is to get a student to take the time to reflect on what he or she has done (process) and has accomplished (product). The following are several student self-evaluation questions that get at the processes of open-ended inquiry such as those that are required in Exploration ILPs:

(1) Did I select a specific phenomenon and focus my attention on it?

(2) Did I find a way to expose its properties (such as through a diagram, sketch, outline, line drawing, or even a description)?

(3) Was I able to "experience" those properties directly or with the help of media?

(4) Can I name the properties that I experienced?

(5) Can I describe the phenomenon and its properties?

The focused inquiry processes required in Competence ILPs can be self-evaluated by students by means of questions such as the following:

(1) Did I identify the competence from "what I needed to be able to do" in order to achieve a goal (such as a tangible article, a personal attribute, a description, a composition, an aesthetic object, an event, or a plan of action)?

(2) Was I able to identify all of the phenomena (the things) that I had to be able to use in performing the competence?

(3) Did I expose the properties of those phenomena that were critical to the performance?

(4) Did I learn how to use those properties for the purpose of achieving my goal?

(5) Do I know the names of those properties?

    (6)   Can I talk about them intelligently?

    (7)   Did I practice performing the competence until I had mastered it?

In addition to such conceptual and process self-evaluation, the student should be helped in both types of Inquiry ILPs to make value judgments about his or her work and to examine the feelings that underlie those values. Questions such as the following are useful for this purpose:

    (1)   Did I choose the topic for this Inquiry ILP or did someone else choose it for me? In either case, was I committed to this inquiry?

    (2)   Was the inquiry interesting for me, or was it dull?

    (3)   Were the plans that I made for studying the phenomenon realistic?

    (4)   What amount of effort did I expend? Great? Modest? Small?

    (5)   Did I learn anything that I did not already know? Very much? Some? None?

To conclude, the evaluation role of the ILP teacher just described is obviously centered on assisting the student to *self*-evaluate his or her own (1) use of basic learning processes, and (2) acquisition of content. Very few teachers were taught this role or the learning processes involved during their pre-service programs. Therefore, as with many new things, it usually takes time, repeated experience, and practice to become comfortable with them. In view of the dividends for learners, however, it *is* worth the effort.

# References
## *(DESIGN FORMAT section)*

Bloom, B. S. (Ed.). *Taxonomy of Educational Objectives, Handbook I: Cognitive Domain.* New York: David McKay Company, Inc., 1956.

Smith, L. W. and P. G. Kapfer. Classroom Management of Learning Package Programs. In *Learning Packages in American Education*, pp. 220-233. Edited by P. G. Kapfer and M. B. Kapfer. Englewood Cliffs, New Jersey: Educational Technology Publications, 1972.

Story Sparkers. Carson, California: Educational Insights, Inc., 1975.

Woodruff, A. D. Analytical Record of Teaching. In *Teacher Education in Transition, Volume I: An Experiment in Change*, pp. 303-306. Edited by Howard E. Bosley. Baltimore, Maryland: Multi-State Teacher Education Project, 1969.

Woodruff, A. D. and J. L. Taylor. A Teaching Behavior Code. In *Teacher Education in Transition, Volume I: An Experiment in Change*, pp. 263-303. Edited by Howard E. Bosley. Baltimore, Maryland: Multi-State Teacher Education Project, 1969.

# IV.

# OUTCOMES

Any instructional design has consequences for both the student and the teacher. The two ILP designs described here promote the following three outcome goals for students: (1) proficiency, (2) confidence, and (3) commitment. These three outcomes will be discussed in the following paragraphs. Subsequently, we will look at outcomes of the ILP approach for the teacher.

## Outcomes for the Student

*Proficiency*. The "proficiency" that results from the use of *Exploration* ILPs is that kind of student familiarity with things and people that allows the student to cope successfully with his environment at his own unique level of development. It is that level of growth that permits the student to know what he or she does *not* know and where to find out about it. It is the fruit of what is commonly referred to as "general education." It is the kind of knowledge that may not necessarily "bring home the bacon," but that is essential as a foundation for vocational or professional specialization.

By way of comparison, the "proficiency" that results from the use of *Competence* ILPs is the ability of a person to do whatever is necessary for achieving a goal. Examples of competencies and their related goals include the following:

(1)    calculating the number of board feet of lumber required for building a house,

(2)    stabilizing the skeletal elements in an injured hand as one step in surgical repair, and

(3)    outlining and ranking major topics and sub-topics while preparing a lecture on new tax legislation to be delivered at a meeting of tax accountants.

*Confidence.* Successful goal attainment, including the attainment of inquiry goals, creates the by-product of confidence. Confidence results when the student is able to gain the competencies which make it possible to succeed in reaching goals that are satisfying to him. Obviously, confidence does not have a curriculum of its own. The school must take into account individual differences among learners by helping each student to evolve goals that he or she values and that are realistic for the student at his or her stage of development.

*Commitment.* Just as there is no curriculum content for confidence outcomes, so there is none for commitment outcomes. Commitments result from a climate of freedom and encouragement for students to examine their own feelings and formulate their own preferences, values, and goals. In addition, the knowledge that students acquire of themselves and their environment helps them to apply rational thinking to the processes of valuing and goal formation.

### Outcomes for the Teacher

*Are ILPs worth it for the teacher?* Whether or not the instructional approaches being advocated in this book are "worth it" for the teacher probably is the wrong question. A more useful question to ask is, "What kind of learning environment will best serve the educational needs of students?" The answer to this question lies in the teacher's view of the aims of education and the nature of behavior and learning. Alternative views are shown in Figure 6 (Woodruff and Kapfer, 1972). Obviously, the authors of this book have opted primarily for the "effective living and doing" orientation, being certain that the "scholarship" and "social conformity" outcomes also will occur at the appropriate times and places to meet individual needs. Exploration and Competence ILPs are designed to help students meet the personal wants of *curiosity satisfacion* and *performance competence.* Both types of ILPs result in personal conceptual knowledge that is so necessary for coping effectively in life.

*ILPs and "open education."* An orientation toward a more "open" kind of education permeates many aspects of the ILP designs presented in this book. Some educators, however, have made the error of assuming that openness in education means license for doing "whatever the students feel like." Actually, open education cannot be achieved without considerable structure, although this may seem at first to be a paradox. The differences between the structure of a conventional curriculum and the structure that makes truly open education possible are critical. Conventional structures do not give the student any significant freedom as to what, why, when, and how he will learn. The simple removal of those conventional structures without adequately substituting some other kind of structure is not the answer, either. What is needed in order for students, teachers, and parents to have access to the freedom for which they are striving are the types of structure that require accountable and responsible behavior.

Some of the structures that make possible student and teacher accountability for learning in all areas of life are the following:

*Figure 6*

*Three Curriculum Orientations*

| **Effective Living** | **Scholarship in a Discipline** | **Social Conformity** |
|---|---|---|
| *The Aim:*<br>To satisfy personal wants. | *The Aim:*<br>To accumulate and organize information. | *The Aim:*<br>To produce an "acceptable" person. |
| *Personal Conceptual Knowledge:*<br>A working familiarity with the behavioral properties of objects in the environment. | *A Disciplined Body of Knowledge:*<br>A body of factual information organized in an orderly structure for storage and retrieval. | *Knowledge of the Social System:*<br>Familiarity with the society, its institutions, its heroes, and its norms. |
| *Life Behavior:*<br>A series of acts consisting of manipulating concrete objects to satisfy personal wants, during which the person develops mental concepts incidental to the personal decisions he makes concerning his own behavior. These concepts then accumulate incidentally into a body of generalized knowledge. | *Academic Behavior:*<br>The systematic search for information required to fill in the cells of an outline. This involves the development of verbal summaries of information about sets of phenomena for the purpose of further inquiry to construct an exhaustive body of such information. | *Social Behavior:*<br>The acceptance of dominant patterns of thought, action and taste, as expressed in daily behavior. |

*(Continued on next page)*

*Figure 6 (Continued)*

**Effective Living**

*A Concept:*

A memory of some of the perceived properties of an object encountered in the environment. Such perceptions or recollections of environmental phenomena are carried within a person and reactivated at decision-points that involve the phenomena.

*Basic Modes of Encounter with Environment:*

Utilization in seeking wants.
(1) Inquiry used to support utilization.
(2) Integration to enhance breadth of understanding.

**Scholarship in a Discipline**

*A Concept:*

The statement of a key idea that is central to an organized body of information. This involves independent packages of data in a file as contrasted with behavioral memories in a person.

*Basic Modes of Encounter with Environment:*

Inquiry and integration.
Systematic processes of data collection and processing to build a disciplined body of information.

**Social Conformity**

*A Concept:*

The key modes of thought of a given social system. A person will have knowledge of the behavioral norms of the institutions of the society.

*Basic Modes of Encounter with Environment:*

Imitation of prevalent patterns in either inquiry behaviors, integration behaviors, or utilization behaviors.

(1)   a structure for exposing the student to the potential curriculum;

(2)   systematic ways to use that structure to keep track of the learnings that are being gained; and

(3)   the use of structured processes that permit the student to expand his or her own goals so that important areas of learning are not ignored through a lack of awareness of their existence.

Even process learning (such as gaining competence in the life-long processes of inquiry) requires structure provided by the teacher during its several formative stages. It also requires structure provided by the student as the competence matures at each stage.

*ILPs and assumptions for teachers*. The use of Exploration and Competence ILPs is based on the following major assumptions, each of which has important implications for the role of the teacher:

(1)   Print and non-print media should be used to facilitate learning in areas in which such materials by themselves are capable of carrying the teaching load.

(2)   Live teachers should be freed from "information dispensing" so that they can concentrate on the kinds of transactions between teacher and learner that are uniquely human and that are essential for efficient learning.

(3)   Attention should be given to insuring the fact that students attain a *functional* level of understanding of the *processes* of learning so that students possess the abilities required for life-long learning and doing.

The first of these three assumptions typically is offered as a reason for designing "independent study" programs. Such programs do free teachers from having to "cover" all of the subject matter content in a course and, thus, such programs contribute to increased efficiency in the use of teaching time. It is obvious that independent study is most certainly a part of the instructional designs represented by Exploration and Competence ILPs.

With the addition of the second assumption, we have moved into an "individualized instructional system." This move requires many more significant changes in both teacher and student roles than does the first assumption. If the teacher is no longer an "information dispenser," then the amount of time needed for total class instruction (whether the class is composed of 30 or 130 students) is greatly reduced. Rather, under an individualized instructional system, teachers and students meet in scheduled seminars and on a "demand" basis during scheduled teacher time.

The third assumption, which is easily recognized as an essential part of both of the Inquiry ILP designs, requires that both teachers and students focus attention on the *processes* that are involved in inquiry. Teachers are interested, of course, in producing students who possess the competencies that they need in life and on the job. In a very rapidly changing world, this means that students at all levels and in every field of endeavor must master the *processes* of open-ended and focused inquiry as well as whatever content is essential at any given point in time.

## Reference
### *(OUTCOMES section)*

Woodruff, A. D. and P. G. Kapfer. Behavioral Objectives and Humanism in Education: A Question of Specificity. *Educational Technology*, January 1972, *12*, 51-55.

# V.

# DEVELOPMENTAL GUIDE

In a sense, this section is a review of the preceding sections of this book. It is a "procedural guide" for developing the Inquiry ILP designs.

## Content Index

The teacher should begin by identifying, extracting, and/or developing a content index for the course or course segment in which ILPs will be used. This may be more difficult than it at first appears, because many textbooks do not provide an adequate outline of content. However, the teacher who is knowledgeable in his or her subject matter field will find many useful standard resources for accomplishing this task.

## Course Requirements

The teacher should specify "required" content, "wouldn't it be nice to know" content, and "it's entirely up to you" content in the content index. Content should be identified for which group experiences will be needed. Lectures, field trips, guest resource persons, etc., for required group teaching-learning experiences should be scheduled. Options should be specified for the *quantity* of work that may be done, and criteria should be determined for assessing the *quality* of student learning. Laboratory and small-group learning activities should be identified. Any required formal evaluations should be scheduled.

### Learning Resources

The teacher should share with the school librarian(s) the planning that he or she has done on the content index and course requirements. These colleagues should be informed regarding what the teacher and his or her students will be doing with media. The teacher should provide as much help as possible to the librarian(s) in selecting print and non-print materials for building a functional collection of resources for individualizing instruction with ILPs. If necessary, the teacher should go so far as to establish guidelines for student movement within and among the classrooms, the learning resource center or library, and the community.

### Learning Stations

The teacher should identify simulated and real work stations where students can apply their focused-inquiry learning. Lecture/demonstration areas, laboratory areas, small-group (discussion) areas, conference times and places, and independent study areas should be scheduled.

### "Training" ILPs

It is obviously impossible to make an instant move into total use of ILPs for inquiry-type learning. Priorities must be set and specifications established for each transition move. Considerable learning about new teacher and student roles must occur along the way.

Whether the teacher plans to emphasize teacher-developed or student-developed ILPs, a sequence of training experiences for students should be planned. These training experiences should employ whatever approach the teacher and students are accustomed to using for getting into something new or different. The teacher should "teach" each part of the ILP formats in whatever amount and detail are appropriate for the experience and maturity of his or her students. In each case, the desired *behavior* (such as writing inquiry questions), the *practice* of that behavior for mastery, and the *evaluation* of that behavior should be congruent. The teacher should remember, in his or her planning, that each inquiry behavior should be initiated in its *simplest appropriate form* before adding other more sophisticated requirements. Formal "inquiry process training" should occur periodically throughout a course or year.

## Recording Learning Outcomes

The teacher should design or adapt the records (to be maintained largely by the students) that will be needed for keeping track of content coverage and the learning of inquiry processes. The student should be helped to obtain feedback for self-evaluation from the following sources:

(1) from the content index, so that the student can determine the adequacy of his content coverage;

(2) from standardized tests, so that the student can compare his general performance on standardized measures with the performance of other students;

(3) from self-tests, so that the student can check on the accuracy of his self-assessments;

(4) from the real world, so that the student can judge the relevance of his learning; and

(5) from faculty and peers, so that frequent concept checking is encouraged.

## Summary

These six procedural steps may be performed by one teacher in a self-contained situation or by teams of teachers working together. These steps are not intended to be absolutely sequential, although there is a certain logic to the order in which they were listed. One thing is certain, however. Once the teacher has discovered, first, the extensive amount of freedom that students can handle if given appropriate structure through ILPs, and second, the rewards of the teacher's new role in an ILP system, the teacher will never again teach in the traditional way. The great burden of "covering the course" will be removed, and much of the responsibility for student learning and student freedom will be where it belongs—with students.

# VI.

# RESOURCES

Individualized Learning Plans (ILPs) have been used in various forms for over a decade. Their development began at the high school level, shortly moved into the middle school level, and then spread rapidly in both directions. Additional descriptive information related to ILP instructional designs is available from the following published sources (unpublished and in-house sources cited earlier are not repeated here):

## BOOKS

Kapfer, Philip G. and Miriam Bierbaum Kapfer. *Project ILPs: Individualized Learning Plans for Life-Based Projects* (Instructional Design Library). Englewood Cliffs, New Jersey: Educational Technology Publications, Inc., 1978.

Kapfer, Philip G. and Miriam Bierbaum Kapfer (Eds.). *Learning Packages in American Education.* Englewood Cliffs, New Jersey: Educational Technology Publications, Inc., 1972. 233 pp.

Kapfer, Philip G., Miriam Bierbaum Kapfer, Asahel D. Woodruff, and Rowan C. Stutz. *Toward the Life-Internship Curriculum.* Carson City, Nevada: Nevada State Department of Education, 1970. 68 pp.

Kapfer, Philip G. and Glen F. Ovard. *Preparing and Using Individualized Learning Packages for Ungraded, Continuous Progress Education.* Englewood Cliffs, New Jersey: Educational Technology Publications, Inc., 1971. 264 pp.

## ARTICLES

Kapfer, Philip G. A Humanistic Theory of Individualized Instruction. *THRUST—for Educational Leadership* (Journal of the Association of California School Administrators), May 1975, *4*, 5-7.

Kapfer, Philip G. An Instructional Management Strategy for Individualizing Learning. *Phi Delta Kappan*, January 1968, *49*, 260-263.

Kapfer, Philip G. Practical Approaches to Individualizing Instruction. *Educational Screen and Audiovisual Guide*, May 1968, *47*, 14-16.

Kapfer, Philip G. and Miriam Bierbaum Kapfer. Introduction to Learning Packages. *Educational Technology*, September 1972, *12*, 9-11.

Kapfer, Philip G., Miriam Bierbaum Kapfer, Asahel D. Woodruff, and Rowan C. Stutz. Realism and Relevance—Payoffs of the Life-Internship Approach. *Educational Technology*, November 1970, *10*, 29-31.

Kapfer, Philip G. and Gardner Swenson. Individualizing Instruction for Self-Paced Learning. *The Clearing House*, March 1968, *42*, 405-410.

Kapfer, Philip G. and William H. Wallin. PACE for Change. *Nevada Education*, Spring 1968, *3*, 8-9 and 28-29.

Kapfer, Philip G. and Asahel D. Woodruff. The Life-Involvement Model of Curriculum and Instruction. *Educational Technology*, September 1972, *12*, 64-72.

Smith, Lucille W. and Philip G. Kapfer. Classroom Management of Learning Package Programs. *Educational Technology*, September 1972, *12*, 80-85.

Woodruff, Asahel D. Cognitive Models of Learning and Instruction. *Instruction: Some Contemporary Viewpoints*, ed. Laurence Siegel. San Francisco, California: Chandler Publishing Company, 1967, 55-98.

Woodruff, Asahel D. The Use of Concepts in Teaching and Learning. *Journal of Teacher Education*, March 1964, *15*, 81-99.

Woodruff, Asahel D. and Philip G. Kapfer. Behavioral Objectives and Humanism in Education: A Question of Specificity. *Educational Technology*, January 1972, *12*, 51-55.

## WORKSHOP

The authors conduct a two-day workshop on ILP approaches.

PHILIP G. KAPFER holds a dual appointment as Research Professor in the Department of Education, Graduate School of Education, and in the Spencer S. Eccles Health Sciences Library at the University of Utah. His divided assignment includes the development of curricular and instructional designs in the public schools and in the health sciences colleges at the University. In addition, Dr. Kapfer serves as Head of the Learning Resource Center at Eccles Library and is a staff member in the Bureau of Educational Research. His current interests are centered on life-based educational programs and the use of computer-assisted instruction. Formerly a chemistry, physics, and mathematics teacher, Dr. Kapfer worked for five years with elementary and secondary teachers in the Clark County School District, Las Vegas, Nevada, on individualization strategies for public school classrooms. He has been a faculty member at the University of Utah since 1970. Dr. Kapfer has published numerous articles and three books and has conducted many workshops on instructional design.

MIRIAM BIERBAUM KAPFER is Research Professor in the Department of Special Education and is on the staff of the Bureau of Educational Research, Graduate School of Education, University of Utah. She is Co-Director of the Life-Involvement Model, and is closely involved with the development of innovative educational programs in the public schools. Her current interests also include instructional designs for exceptional children and the arts. Dr. Kapfer is an expert on the use of behavioral objectives in curriculum development, having edited a book on that topic in 1971. Formerly a music and English teacher at the elementary and secondary levels, Dr. Kapfer also worked as Research Specialist in the Clark County School District, Las Vegas, Nevada, prior to coming to the University of Utah. Dr. Kapfer has published many articles and three books on various aspects of the broad field of educational planning.